**W9-AYR-730**

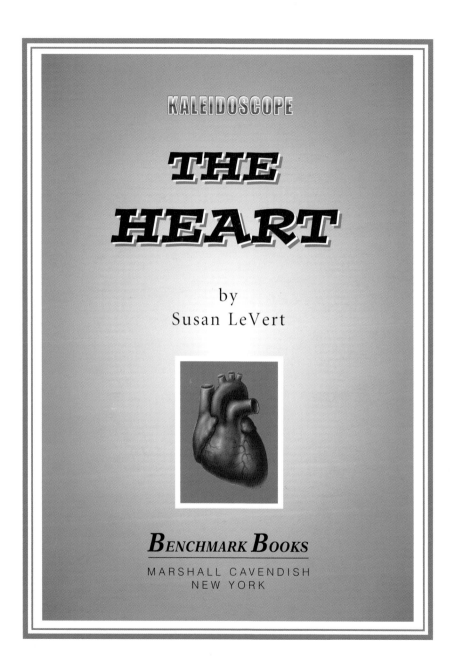

KALEIDOSCOPE

# THE
# HEART

by
Susan LeVert

**BENCHMARK BOOKS**

MARSHALL CAVENDISH
NEW YORK

Benchmark Books
Marshall Cavendish Corporation
99 White Plains Road
Tarrytown, New York 10591-9001
Website: www.marshallcavendish.com

Library of Congress Cataloging-in-Publication Data
LeVert, Suzanne, date
The heart / by Suzanne LeVert.
    p.cm. – (Kaleidoscope)
Includes bibliographical references and index.
ISBN 0-7614-1306-5
1. Heart—Juvenile literature. [1. Heart.] I. Title. II. Series.
QP111.6 .L48 2001      612.1'7—dc21      00-050727

Photo Research by Anne Burns Images

Cover Photo: Alex Grey/Peter Arnold, Inc.

The photographs in this book are used by permission and through the courtesy of: *Phototake: Image Shop/Phototake NYC,* 5.
John Karrapelou,CMI, 13. *Photo Researchers: Francis LeRoy, Biocosmos/Science Photo Library,* 6; *MVI/Science Source,* 9, 10;
Science Photo Library, 17. Matt Meadows/ Science Photo Library, 22; Dr. Gopal Murti/Science Photo Library, 25. Meckes/Ottawa/
Eye of Science, 29; Oliver Meckes, 30; Dept. of Clinical Radiology, Salisbury Districk Hospital/Science Photo Library, 33; John Bavosi/
Science Photo Library, 37, 38; Erick Schrempp, 34. *Peter Arnold:* Steve Allen: 14; Manfred Kage, 18; Leonard Lessin, 21;
David M. Phillips, 26. *Photo Edit, Meryleen Ferguson,* 41; Felicia Martin, 42.

Printed in Italy

6 5 4 3 2 1

# CONTENTS

# THE BEAT OF YOUR HEART

With your right hand, make a fist. Consider its size. That's about the size of the organ inside your chest called the heart. The heart is made of some of the most powerful muscle tissue in the body.

Squeeze your fist hard and hold it for about a second. Now release it. Your heart performs an action like this some sixty to eighty times a minute, twenty-four hours a day, seven days a week, for your whole life. The number of times your heart beats per minute is called your heart rate, or pulse. The faster you move or the harder you work, the faster and harder your heart works to bring more blood to your muscles, brain, and other parts of your body.

*The heart is a fist-sized muscular organ that sits within your chest.*

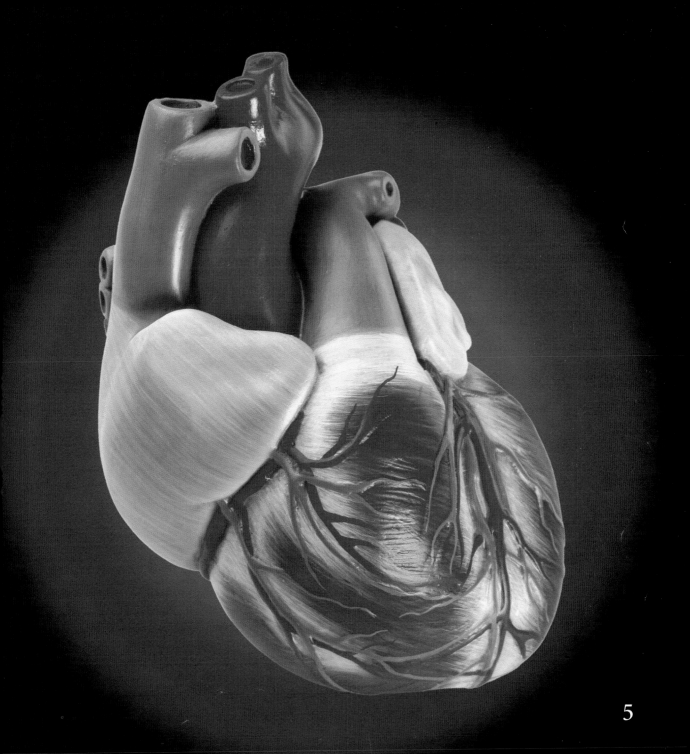

5

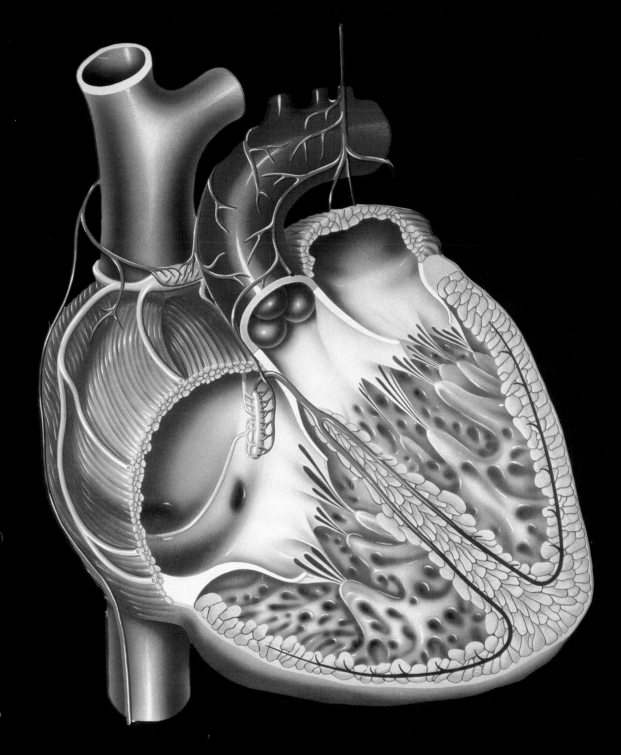

6

Every time your heart squeezes together and releases, it acts like a pump. This pump pushes blood that has collected within it out into the lungs or to the rest of the body. In fact, the heart actually works as two matched pumps: one on the right side of the heart and the other on the left side. Each side has a top and a bottom chamber.

The two top chambers (called the right atrium and the left atrium) hold blood coming into the heart. The two bottom chambers (called the right ventricle and the left ventricle) hold blood going out of the heart. Valves open and close to let blood in and out of these chambers. Let's take a closer look at how this all works.

*The internal structure of the heart. Note the right and left atria on top, and the right and left ventricles on the bottom.*

# IN A HEARTBEAT

Each heartbeat has three phases:

1. Blood filled with oxygen enters the left atrium while at the very same time, deoxygenated blood enters the right atrium.

2. Both *atria contract,* which squeezes the blood through the valves and into the *ventricles* below.

*The three phases of a heartbeat.*

# THE FLOW OF BLOOD

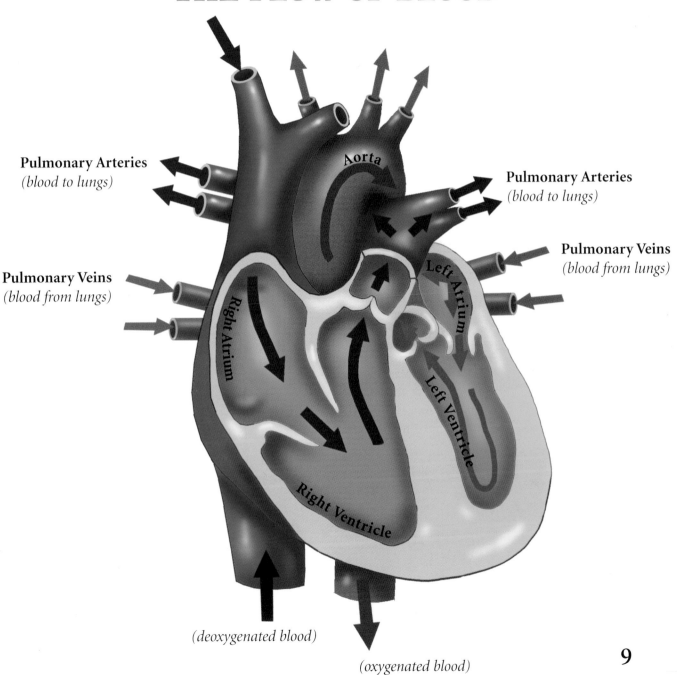

**Pulmonary Arteries**
*(blood to lungs)*

**Pulmonary Veins**
*(blood from lungs)*

Aorta

**Pulmonary Arteries**
*(blood to lungs)*

**Pulmonary Veins**
*(blood from lungs)*

Right Atrium

Left Atrium

Left Ventricle

Right Ventricle

*(deoxygenated blood)*

*(oxygenated blood)*

9

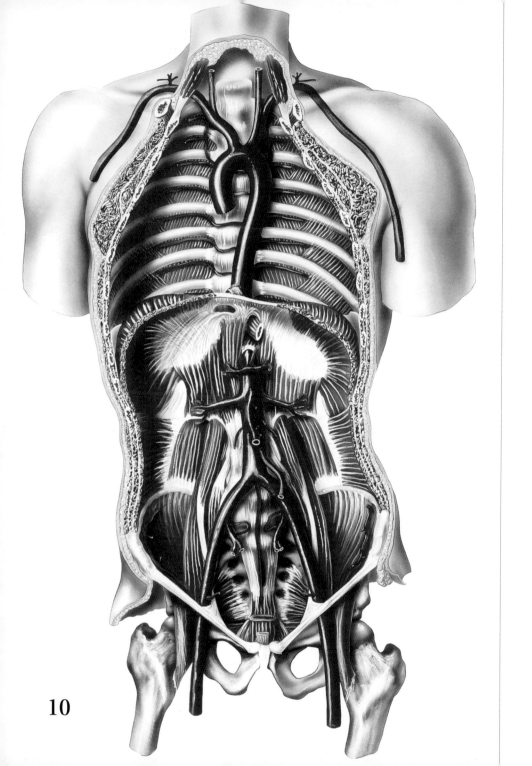

10

3. Finally, the ventricles contract, which forces the valves to open. From the right ventricle, blood flows into the pulmonary artery and to the lungs. From the left ventricle, blood enters the aorta, the large vessel that leads away from the heart.

The whole cycle lasts only about four fifths of a second and involves about six tablespoons of blood.

The regular rhythm of your heartbeat is maintained by electrical impulses.

*The aorta is the hook-shaped artery at the top of the illustration. It is the largest blood vessel in the body. It supplies oxygen-rich blood to all other arteries.*

# THE HEART IS ELECTRIC

In the heart, a special tissue called the *pacemaker* sends out these impulses. The impulses flow along muscle fibers and trigger the ventricles to contract. The pacemaker receives its messages from the *vagus nerve,* which starts out in the brain. The vagus nerve maintains the heart rate at about sixty to seventy beats per minutes unless the brain signals it to speed up when you're exercising or under stress. When the heart rate speeds up, it sends even more blood into the vessels and then to other parts of the body.

*A comparison of active and sedentary hearts.*

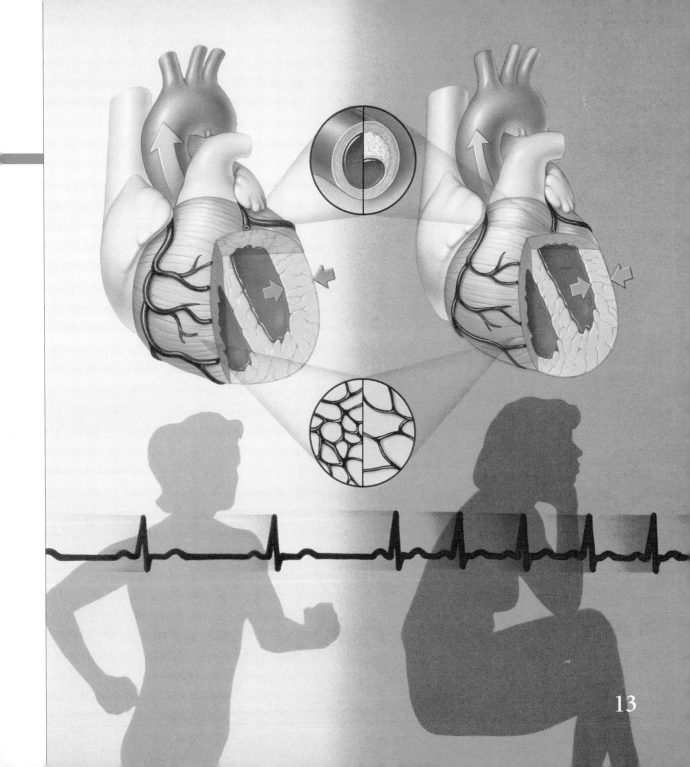

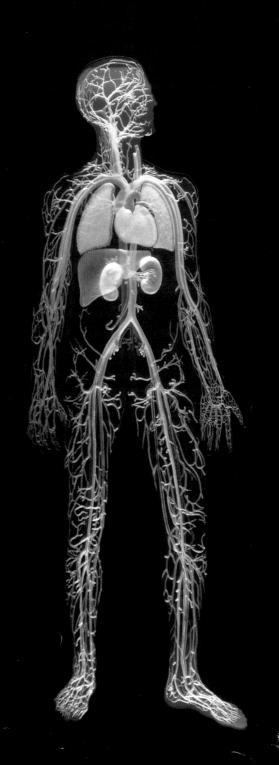

# ROUND AND ROUND WE GO

The heart, along with a huge network of large, small, and very tiny tubes called vessels, make up the circulatory system. The vessels carry blood to and from the heart to every single cell in the body.

Blood contains oxygen from the air you breath, vitamins and minerals from the food you eat, and other important materials your cells need to thrive. This system is ninety thousand miles long, but it only takes blood one minute to complete a full *circuit*.

*Believe it or not, a drop of blood can travel from your heart through your entire body and back again in about one minute.*

# THE POWER OF YOUR VESSELS

When your heart pumps, the blood going away from the heart first flows through the biggest vessel in the body, which is called the aorta. The aorta branches out into smaller tubes called arteries. Your arteries split into smaller and smaller tubes to reach every part of your body—from the brain to the tips of your toes. The tiniest *arteries* are called capillaries. They bring oxygen, water, and other nutrients to the organs and tissues in the body. They also bring blood to the surface of your skin when you get hot, which is why your face turns red when you overheat! Blood travels pretty fast when it's in your arteries—about twelve inches per second.

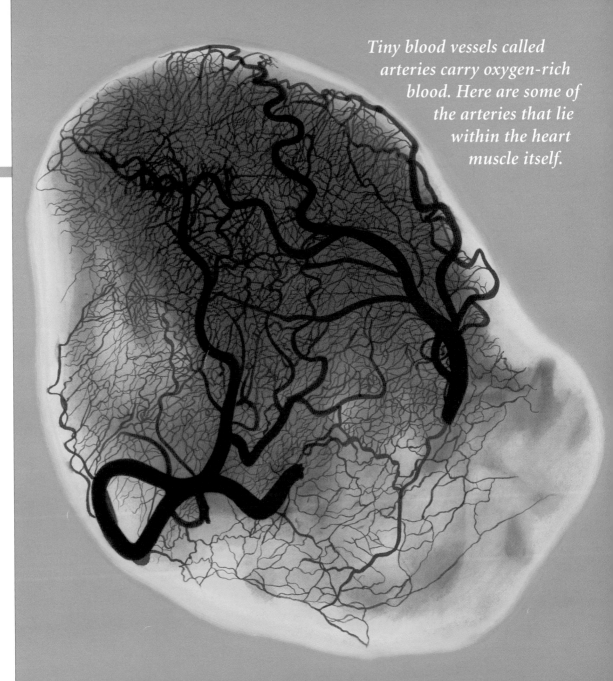

*Tiny blood vessels called
arteries carry oxygen-rich
blood. Here are some of
the arteries that lie
within the heart
muscle itself.*

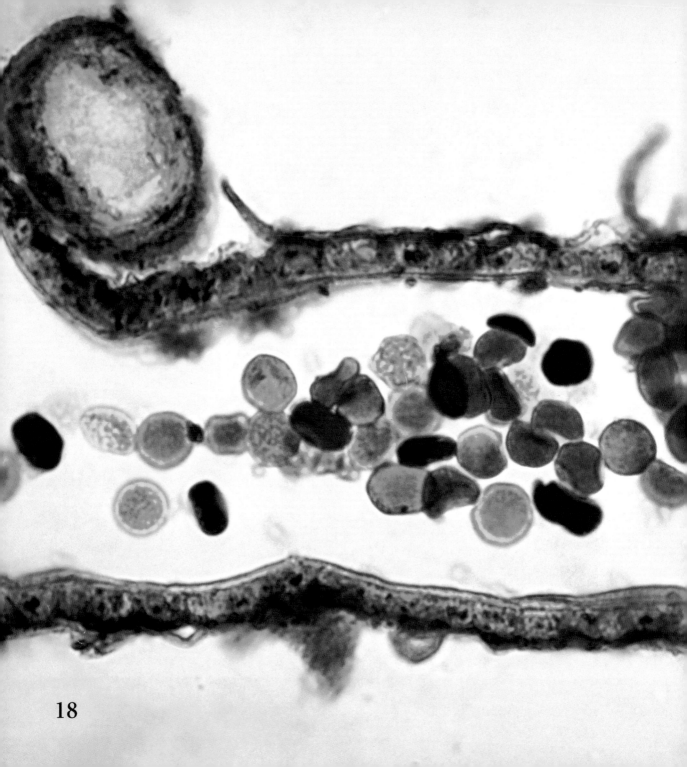

18

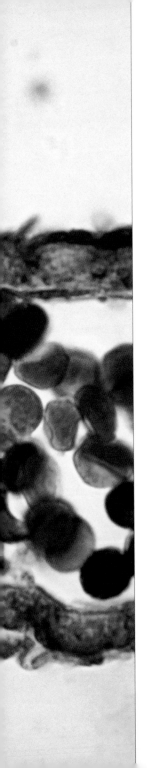

Through the thin capillary walls, the blood drops off oxygen to the cells and picks up the waste gas carbon dioxide. Then the blood starts its return trip to the heart through the veins.

*Capillaries are the smallest blood vessels. Their walls are so thin that oxygen and other nutrients are able to pass through them and enter the cells of organs in the body.*

19

Take a look at your hand. See the bluish-colored lines? Those are a few of your veins, which are part of the network of vessels that carry your blood back to your heart. The blood in these vessels looks blue because it carries less oxygen. Blood travels through your veins at the rate of about eight inches per second.

Now let's take a closer look at your blood and what it does.

*The veins on the back of your hand help carry blood to your heart.*

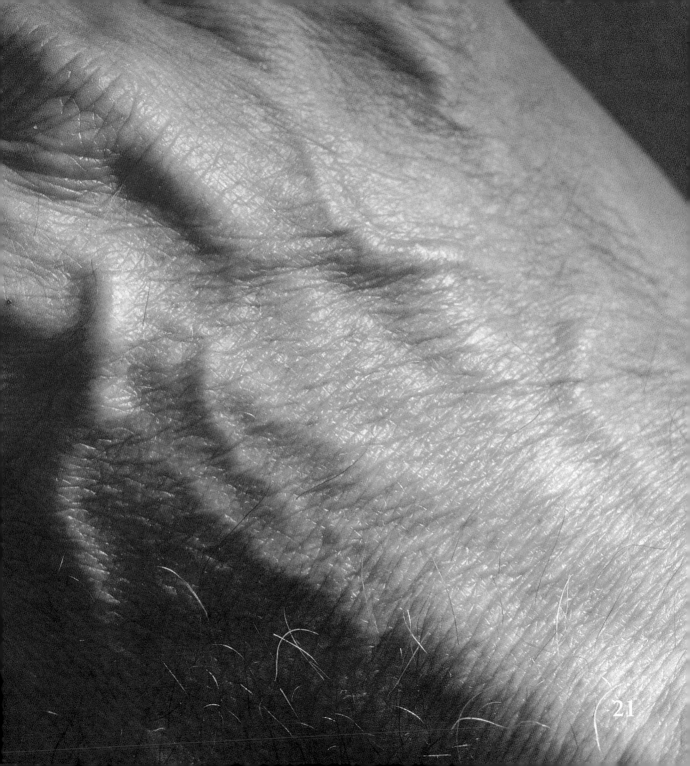

21

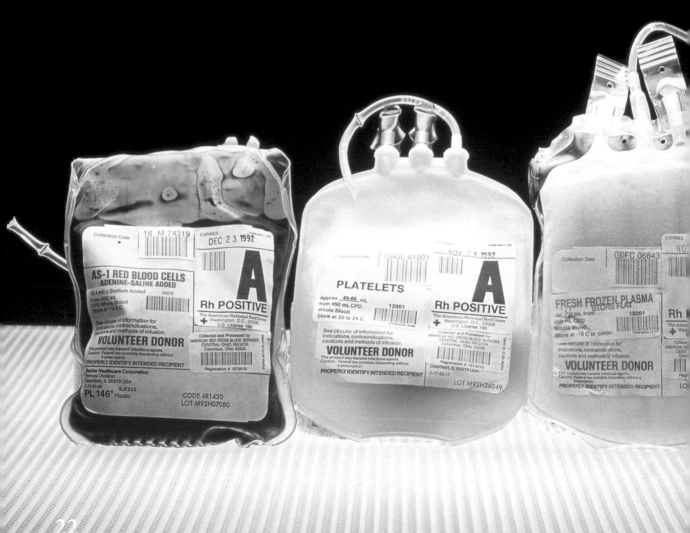

# THE RICHNESS OF YOUR BLOOD

If you've ever cut your finger or scraped your knee, you've seen what blood looks like when it's outside the body. It's bright red and feels very sticky. You have a lot of blood in your body: The average ten-year-old has about six pints of blood—enough to fill a three-quart milk carton. An adult has about ten pints.

*Your blood contains many different substances, including red blood cells (at the right), the liquid portion of the blood, called plasma (to the far left), and large blood cells called platelets that help the blood to clot (center).*

Blood serves many different purposes in the body. Most of your blood is made up of a yellowish liquid called *plasma*. Plasma takes nutrients from the food you eat and delivers them to the cells of your body. Plasma also takes waste products from the cells to the kidneys. The kidneys wash the waste products out of the body with urine.

*Plasma cells help bring nutrients to the other cells of the body and carry away waste products.*

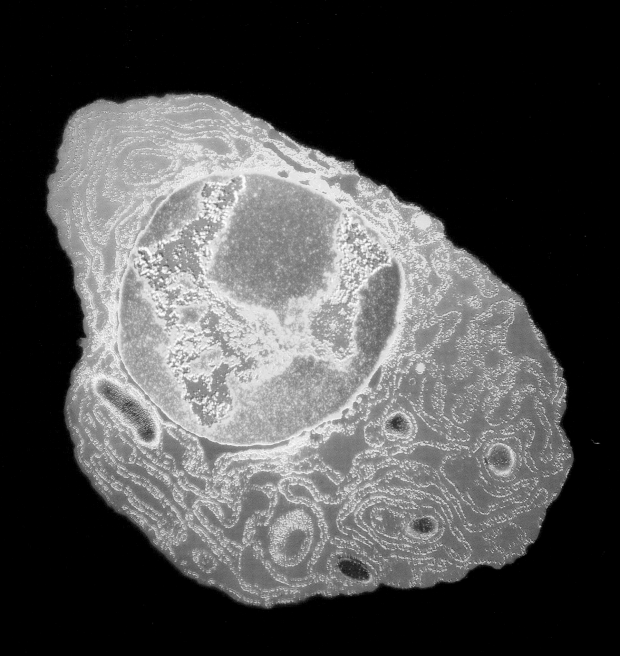

Red blood cells are the largest components of blood. Without them, our bodies would not receive the oxygen and nutrients they need for survival.

# THE BREATH OF LIFE

Red blood cells carry oxygen and other nutrients to the cells of the body. As they give up their oxygen, red blood cells collect carbon dioxide, which they carry back to your lungs. Every time you exhale (breathe out), you rid your body of the carbon dioxide.

Red blood cells don't live very long in the body—only about 80 to 120 days. Two million red blood cells die every second. New ones are created by bone marrow, special tissue located inside your bones.

What gives your red blood cells their color is a protein called *hemoglobin.* Oxygen from the lungs enters the red blood cells and combines with hemoglobin, which allows the blood to transport oxygen to the cells. The cells use oxygen as energy.

White blood cells fight germs and other poisons. They have special markers on their membranes (skinlike coverings) that attach to germs and destroy them. If your body is attacked by a lot of germs, it makes extra white blood cells to fight them off.

*White blood cells are part of your immune system. They help your body fight off disease and infection. Here, a white blood cell attacks E. coli bacteria cells.*

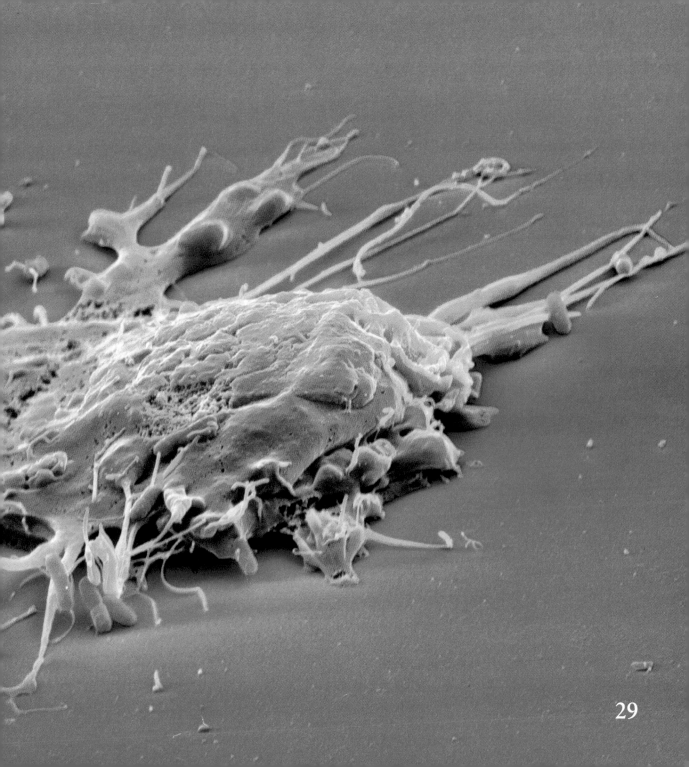

29

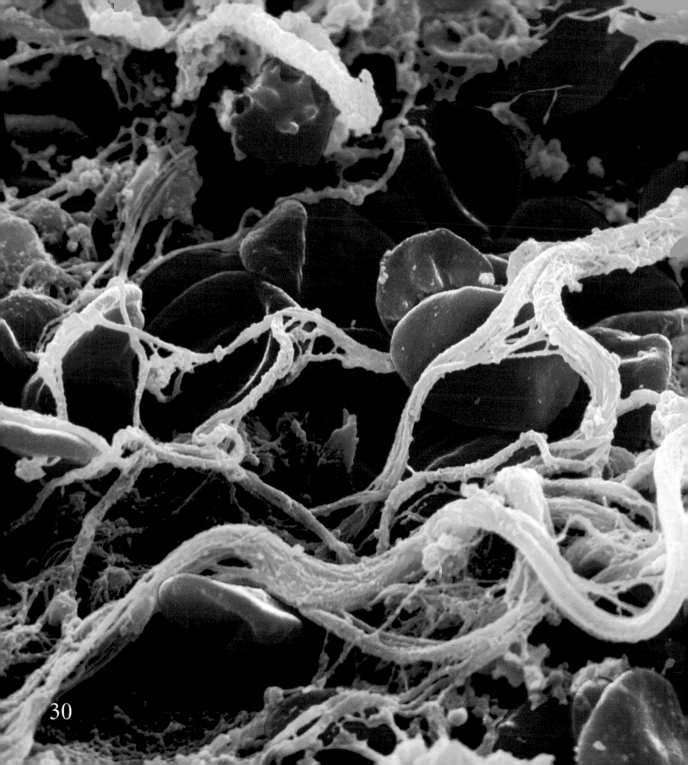

30

Other cells can clot, or solidify, to stop the blood from flowing when you cut yourself. The clot then dries into a scab, which falls off when new skin has grown underneath. If you bump yourself, a bruise will form when blood leaks into your skin.

*Your blood contains substances that help to heal wounds. Here, yellow bands of fibrin hold back red blood cells to form a clot.*

# WHAT CAN GO WRONG

The circulatory system usually does all of its work automatically. But some people have problems that upset this work. Here are a few things that can go wrong:

• The nervous system can fail to send the right impulses to regulate the heartbeat. When it doesn't, the heart might skip a beat, beat too fast, or beat too slow. Doctors use electronic devices called artificial pacemakers to reestablish the right rhythm.

• Sometimes the heart isn't formed right, often because of something that happens before birth. If the problem lies in the valves, the doctor can hear a heart murmur, which is the sound of blood rushing the wrong way. Surgery can repair most of these defects and people with them then live normal, healthy lives.

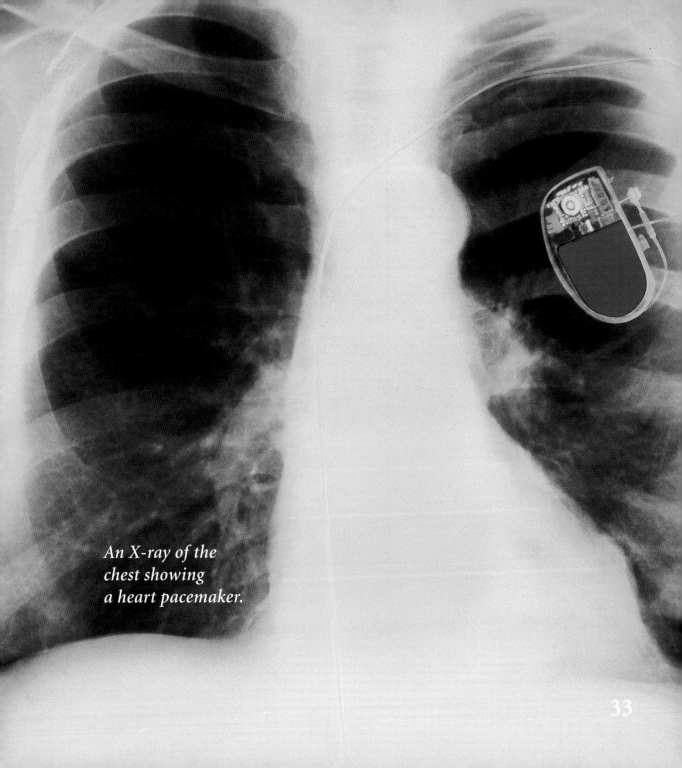

*An X-ray of the chest showing a heart pacemaker.*

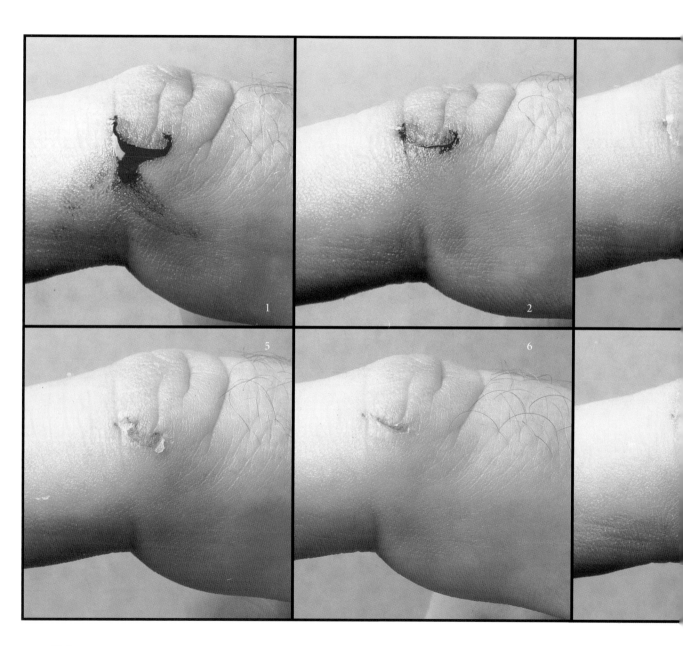

34

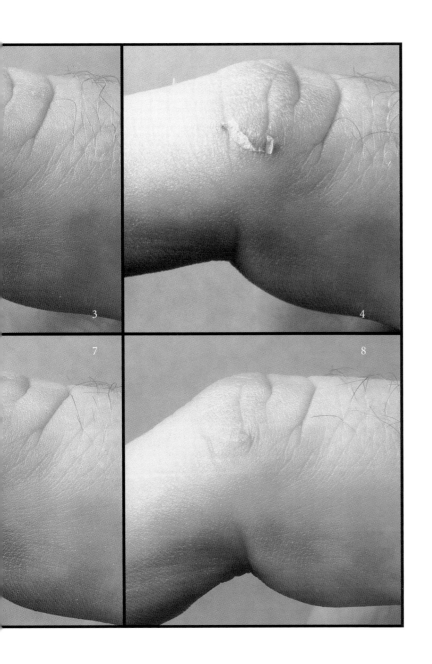

• Blood can fail to clot (a condition called hemophilia) or doesn't contain enough iron to carry oxygen (a condition called anemia).

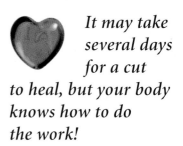

*It may take several days for a cut to heal, but your body knows how to do the work!*

• Blood can flow through the vessels under pressure that's too high, a condition called high blood pressure or hypertension. The high pressure can cause damage to the vessels, leading to serious health problems, including heart attacks.

*In order to carry blood throughout the body, your blood vessels should be clean and clear. When the arteries become clogged with fat and scar tissue, serious problems, such as heart attack and stroke, can occur.*

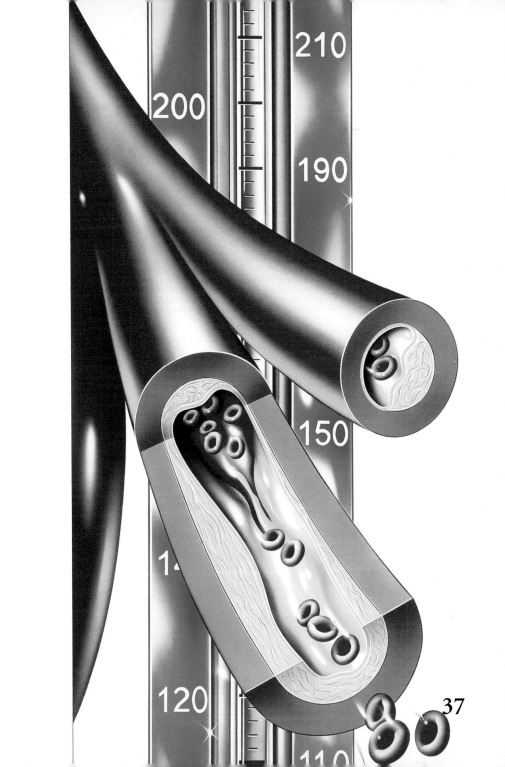

210

200

190

150

14

120

37

110

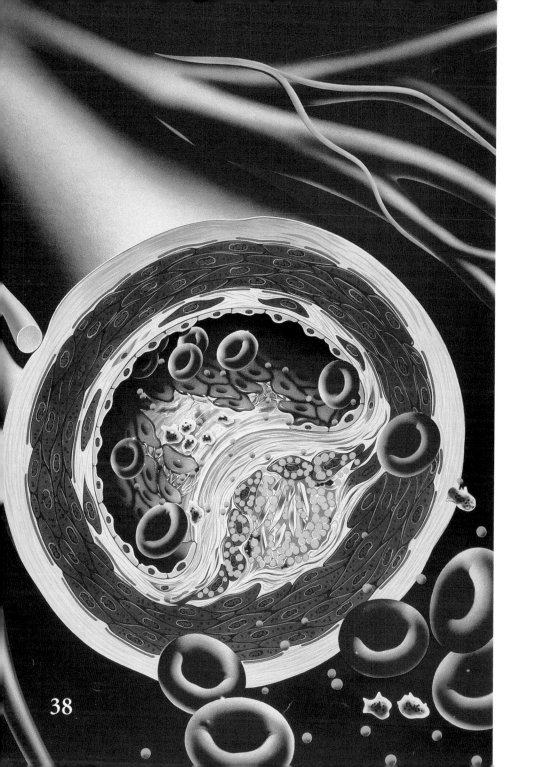

• A heart attack occurs when heart tissue dies due to a lack of oxygen. Most heart problems are referred to as coronary heart disease. The arteries leading from the heart can get clogged up with fat and other material. If they become so clogged, the heart tissue can't receive enough blood from the artery. This is called a heart attack. Heart attacks are the most common cause of death in the United States today.

*You can see how narrow and clogged this artery is, making it difficult for blood to pass through.*

# How to Keep Your Heart Pumping and Your Blood Flowing

Now that you know that your heart is a muscle, you can keep it healthy. And to do that, you need to exercise. Just like you need to work the muscles in your legs to keep them strong, you need to exercise your heart so that it stays healthy. You can best exercise your heart by running, jumping, dancing, and riding your bike. These activities will make the heart pump harder, which will strengthen the muscle that keeps it pumping.

*Exercise is one way of keeping your heart healthy.*

41

The other thing you can do to keep your heart and blood vessels healthy is to eat a healthy diet. That means avoiding fatty foods such as French fries and cheeseburgers, and eating plenty of vegetables and fresh fruit. Fat can clog and damage blood vessels while the fiber, vitamins, and minerals in vegetables and fruit can help keep them clear and strong.

Remember, you're going to need your heart and your blood vessels for the rest of your life.

*A healthy diet provides the basic nutrients your heart and your whole body need to stay strong and vital.*

43

# GLOSSARY

**Arteries**  Smooth, elastic tubes that transport blood away from the heart to all other parts of the body.

**Atria**  The top two chambers of the heart.

**Circuit**  The complete, enclosed path the blood vessels take from the heart to every organ and cell in the body and back.

**Contract**  Close together.

**Hemoglobin**  The protein in red blood cells that combines with oxygen, carrying it from the lungs throughout the body.

**Pacemaker**  A group of cells in the heart that sends electrical impulses that signal the heart to beat in a regular rhythm. If this group of cells fails to work, doctors to implant an artificial pacemaker to do the work.

**Plasma**   The liquid part of the blood that contains proteins, salts, and other nutrients.

**Vagus nerve**   A nerve cell in the brain that helps control automatic functions like the beat of the heart.

**Ventricles**   The two bottom chambers of the heart.

# FIND OUT MORE

BOOKS:

Gregson, Susan R. *Heart Disease (Perspectives on Disease and Illness)* Mankato, MN: Lifematters, 2001

Hurst, J. Willis, Stuart Hurst, Jackie Ball, Patricia J. Wynne. *The Heart: The Kids' Question and Answer Book.* New York: McGraw-Hill. 1998.

Simon, Seymour. *The Heart: Our Circulatory System.* New York: Morrow Junior Books, 1999.

WEBSITES:

Kids Health
http://www.kidshealth.org/kid/body/heart_SW.html

The Virtual Body
http://www.medtropolis.com/vbody/

# AUTHOR'S BIO

Suzanne LeVert is a writer and editor of young adult and trade books with more than 30 titles to her credit. Although she specializes in health topics, Suzanne also enjoys writing about history and politics and is the author of *Louisiana* and *Massachusetts* in the Benchmark Books series, Celebrate the States. Suzanne currently lives in New Orleans, Louisiana and attends Tulane Law School.

# INDEX

*Page numbers for illustrations are in boldface.*